Rituals
&
Icebreakers

Practical tools for
forming community

Rituals
&
Icebreakers

Practical tools for
forming community

Kathleen O'Connell Chesto

Liguori
ONE LIGUORI DRIVE
LIGUORI MO 63057-9999

ISBN 0-7648-0407-3
Library of Congress Catalog Card Number: 98-75394

© 1999, Kathleen O'Connell Chesto
Printed in the United States of America
04 05 06 07 08 6 5 4 3 2

To order, call 1-800-325-9521
www.liguori.org

Cover design by Ross M. Sherman
Interior illustrations by Kathleen Chesto and Vicki Breashears

Contents

II. Rituals

to all the people

who have ever been "on FIRE"

Introduction

The hunger for community is an overwhelming feature of to-day's society. We gather in groups that promise to "support" us in anything from losing weight to dealing with death. There is a support group somewhere for every ache expressed by the human spirit and some for those we have yet to voice. In asking group after group around the North American continent what they hope for from their churches, the first response I receive is always "community."

Yet, I have found very few churches that actually succeed in becoming community. Part of the problem is often size; it is difficult to be community where no one knows your name. Part of the problem rests with the individuals who want community to miraculously happen to them, without the struggle and the pain that true community always involves. And part of the problem is the rugged individualism so much a part of the American spirit, an individualism that tells us we should be able to do everything on our own. Becoming a community implies being vulnerable, and many of us are simply not willing to take that risk.

According to M. Scott Peck, community is a group of individuals who have learned how to communicate honestly with each other, whose relationships go deeper than their masks of composure, who have developed some significant commitment to rejoice together, mourn together, delight in each other. Such a community is inherently mysterious, a whole that is more than the sum of its parts, people drawn together by crisis, common need, a shared moment, or perhaps just by chance.[1]

---

1. M. Scott Peck. *The Different Drum* (New York: Simon and Schuster, 1987).

Most churches of several hundred families have already discovered that becoming a community with "significant commitment" and "deeper relationships" requires starting with small groups within which these relationships are possible. Our first community was a small group of families, drawn together by "common need," the need to hand on our faith tradition to our children in an environment that supported that faith, with people who shared our moral and spiritual commitment. We discovered that even an intense devotion to a common task is not enough to create a community. Communities may be drawn together by accident or chance; they take time and attention to survive and grow.

The religious education program, FIRE, that grew out of that first group of families, has been struggling for 19 years to help other families develop support communities for handing on faith. This book is not intended as a treatise on community-building or an exploration of the phases a group passes through on its way to becoming community. It is a simple effort to provide groups, particularly those with a wide span of ages, with tools we have discovered were necessary in developing certain aspects of community. None of the games or rituals, and no amount of strict adherence to playing and praying, will "create" community, any more than flour and eggs can create a cake. These ingredients are offered with the hope of making the group's task easier as it struggles to become community.

The book has been divided into two sections to make it easier to use. The first section offers *icebreakers:* games for learning names, games for getting to know one another better, games for learning to work and play together. While these games were developed primarily by FIRE groups throughout the United States and Canada, many of the suggestions have been used successfully with Scouts, PTA's, youth ministry programs, 4-H, and various catechetical programs and retreats.

The second section is on *rituals,* ideas for enabling communities to pray together. It begins with a reflection on the use of symbol in the development of ritual prayer and directions for making and using specific symbols within a group. The remainder of the book is comprised of two sets of rituals. Rituals in the first set celebrate general themes, seasons, and ideas, with directions for using a concrete symbol. The second set of rituals focuses on the more specific themes represented by the symbols described earlier and are cross-referenced with these symbols for easier use. While the rituals were designed for beginning and closing meetings or classes, most can be expanded into prayer services that stand alone.

What we discovered in FIRE was that the heart of the lesson is never the experience, the feedback, or the prayer; it is the community. If we neglected to develop that community, we limited FIRE to a religious education program that teaches doctrine to families. To neglect to develop community in any group that meets within our churches, from youth ministry programs to adult education, is to limit that group to accomplishing a task and to deprive it of a potential experience of church.

1

ICEBREAKERS

Every group that gathers brings with it its own fears and prejudices. There is a tendency for new group members to enter with their guard up, seeing themselves as separate and different from the others, sitting in judgment, to some extent, on the personhood of others. Before anything of strong lasting value can take place, some of those walls need to be broken down.

This is the process of "icebreaking." It is an excellent word because the image it conveys is exactly what we are trying to accomplish. Icebreakers chop through the hardened surface of built-in fears and frozen misconceptions. First they leave the chunks of ice free to bump up against one another, wear down some of the rougher edges, and even exchange places in the water. Eventually, enough of the ice is broken into small enough chunks to allow the water to flow freely, carrying the remaining ice flows away in the flood.

The more resistant a group is to icebreakers, the more in need they are of the process.

A COMMUNITY IS WHERE EVERYONE KNOWS YOUR NAME

A community is where everyone knows your name. Being called by name empowers us. You are not "one of the Smith's"; you are "Emily," unique, different, special. Scripture tells us over and over again the importance of name. Isaiah says: "I have called you by name and you are mine." (Is 43:1b) Calling someone by name implies a connectedness, a belonging to one another. Any group that hopes to become a community needs to pay careful attention to this fact and be willing to devote the time it takes to get to know everyone by name.

Of equal importance is naming the group. A group that has no name will always be known by the leader's name, as in "I belong to Kathy Chesto's group." Simply by making such a statement, the speaker places the responsibility and ownership for the group solely on the leader's shoulders. By naming the group, and allowing everyone some voice in choosing the name, the responsibility is extended to the group as a whole. The name can be as simple as a number or Greek letter, or as complex as a scripture reference. I have been in parishes where all the groups in a renewal program were numbered, and I have heard community names as varied as "Voyagers," "Fireworks," "Beehive," and "Happiness Is. . . ." "I belong to the Beehive" carries in the very statement a sense of ownership missing when we name a group by the leader.

Naming a group involves the struggle to understand the meaning and purpose this community has for those within it. It is a symbolic act of assigning significance to a group that may not, as yet, have experienced its own significance.

3

Owning the name usually proves to be a far longer process than simply designating it.

The task of learning members' names is less complex but often more demanding. It requires attentiveness. Creating an atmosphere where everyone is free to call each person by name also involves vulnerability and risk.

The following games are designed for learning—and remembering!—names. Some of them may seem silly, and adults may, at first, feel foolish playing them. They are a leveling force in any community, asking us to be willing to risk surrendering a little of our self-assurance in order to be truly known by others. All of them can be played several times, and most are more enjoyable the second or third time through.

Don't be afraid to spend several weeks learning names. Most people will be grateful to be reminded. Adults have a particularly difficult time with the names of children because our society allows them to be dismissed as lesser members of a family. Knowing everyone's name will not make a group into a community, but not knowing names will certainly prevent a group from becoming one.

Yarn Web

---◆---

Group size: 10-40. The game is uninteresting with too small a group, and boring and cumbersome with too large a group.

Group age: Intergenerational

Materials: A large ball of yarn

Purpose: Learning names

---◆---

Directions:

The leader begins holding a large ball of yarn. The leader says her name and something she particularly likes that begins with the same sound. For example, "My name is Kathy and I like cookies." It is important to use the same *sound* rather than the same letter, since younger children in the group will not know how to spell.

As the leader speaks, she grasps the end of the yarn and throws the ball to someone else in the group. The second person grabs the yarn, pulling it taut with the leader, gives his name and something he likes that begins with the same sound, and tosses the yarn ball to someone else.

The game continues until everyone has been thrown the ball and is holding a piece of the yarn. (It is necessary to remind people frequently before they throw the ball, to hold on to the yarn.) The yarn will form a web across the center of the group.

The leader should then tug on the yarn, demonstrating that everyone can feel the pull. In a community, what affects one of us affects all of us. The web is distorted if any member drops an end, but the community can still support it.

If there is extra time, the community can try to unweave the web by having the last person throw the yarn ball back to the person from whom it was caught, naming the person and what she likes. This is far more difficult than it sounds: the yarn can get badly tangled if the ball drops, but it can be fun!

When the group knows names a little better, the game can be repeated, having the person who throws the ball name the person to whom it is thrown.

What's My Number?

---◆---

Group size: 10 or more. (The larger the group, the longer the game can go on.)

Group age: This can be done with anyone old enough to write, or with intergenerational groups having younger members by pairing those children with an adult.

Materials: Slips of paper, each containing a different number, enough for each person in the group to have one; common pins; paper and pencils

Purpose: Learning names

---◆---

Directions:

As each person enters the meeting, the leader and one or two helpers pin a number on the person's back. Each person also receives a pencil and paper. Ask people to sit immediately, so they are not revealing their numbers before they know how to play the game.

The idea of the game is to find out everyone's number while not revealing your own. When a participant sees a person's number, he writes the person's name and number on the slip of paper. If the participant is not old enough to write, she can work in partnership with an adult, as long as she is old enough to recognize numerals. Children are actually very good at sneaking behind people and discovering numbers. However, it is not fair to carry a child piggyback with the intent of hiding the bearer's number.

Once the rules have been explained, ask everyone to stand up and "mill about," trying to keep their numbers secret. They are allowed to pair up with someone, if they choose to do so. Allow about 10 minutes for the game. Participants must ask members' names if they don't know them. The person who has the most correct names and numbers on her list wins.

Don't be surprised if the less-competitive in the group make no effort to win, or focus on helping a child. The idea is to have fun and learn people's names. Any way that works for the group is fine.

Teens are particularly fond of this game and will play longer and more intensely than a group of mixed ages. They will have fun with it long after they know everyone's name.

NOAH'S ARK

---◆---

Group size: *10-50. You are actually only limited by the number of animals you can name. You can play the game in groups, instead of pairs, if you run out of animals.*

Group age: *Intergenerational*

Materials: *One index card for each person in the group, the name of an animal on each card. Every animal must appear on two cards, if you are playing in pairs, or on several cards if you have over 50 people and you are playing in large groups.*

Purpose: *Having fun, learning names*

---◆---

Directions (playing in pairs):

As each person comes in, give her a card with an animal name on it and ask her to keep it a secret. Make SURE that you have two of each animal. If you have an odd number of people in your group, the leader should balance it off by playing or not playing, as needed. Try to make sure that people in the same family do not get the same animal. It is also possible to hand the names out just before you begin to play. Designate an area of the room as Noah's Ark.

Instruct everyone to make a noise or a motion, or both, to indicate the animal each has. All must get up and move around the room doing this until they find their partner animals. Once they find their partners, they go and stand in Noah's Ark and continue to make the noise or motion. When everyone is in the ark, talk briefly about how cramped and smelly it must have gotten after 40 days. Everyone was anxious to get off.

To leave the ark, members must be able to introduce each other to the group. They leave together and go sit down.

For Group Playing:

In large groups, give several people the names of the same animal. They must begin to make noise. As they find their like animals, they continue to move through the group, collecting all the dogs, cats, pigs, or whatever. When they are certain that all have been found, they move to the side of the room and continue to make their noise. The object is to finish first and have fun, making enough noise to confuse the others.

This variation works best in a large parish hall.

I'VE GOT YOUR NUMBER

---◆---

Group size: 16-50. *There must be an even number of people. The leader should play or not play, as needed.*

Group age: Intergenerational

Materials: A small piece of paper for each person in the group. One numeral is written on each paper, each numeral is written twice.

Purpose: Getting to know each other better

---◆---

Directions:

Before the group arrives, the leader chooses a fact she wants the people of the group to learn about each other. If the group is fairly new, choose something simple such as: favorite color, favorite music, favorite sport, worst food, etc. Each person is given a number as he enters. There are *two* of each numeral. Make sure people in the same family do not get matching numbers. The object is to find the other person with your number. However, before you are allowed to ask anyone her number, you must first ask the person's name and the particular fact decided in advance by the leader. As soon as the match is made, both people sit down. When everyone is sitting, pairs introduce each other to the group and give the person's response to the "favorite" question.

If your group has been meeting for some time and you are certain that all the names are known, you can ask a tougher question, such as "Name one thing that really makes you angry," before you ask the person's number. This information can then be shared with the group. Do not, however, assume prematurely that all names are known.

FACT FIND

---◆---

Group size: *15+*

Group age: *Members need to be able to read. In intergenerational groups, small children or those who have difficulty reading can be partnered with parents or other adults. Or the game can be played in teams.*

Materials: *A list of 20 facts for each person. People should all be given the same list, with a space for writing a name after each fact, e.g.,*

Hates chocolate _____
Got an A in math _____
Likes country music_____
Has a cat _____
Can't swim_____
Plays flute _____
Favorite meal is breakfast_____
Watches "General Hospital" _____
etc. (Include things specific to your group.)

Purpose: *Learning names, getting to know each other better*

---◆---

Directions:

Everyone is given a list of facts as the meeting begins. The object of the game is to find a person who fits each fact. Each person may only be used once. The group is given 5-7 minutes to find the right people. Time is called before anyone gets all 20. The person who was able to match the most items wins. Be sure to check for accuracy by having the winner read facts and names aloud. If there are teenagers, have a prize that can be shared by the family, like a gift certificate for hamburgers or pizza.

People Bingo

Group size: 15+ *(This has been done successfully with several hundred people.)*

Group age: *This game also requires reading ability, but little ones can be teamed with adults. This game also works well with adults only.*

Materials: *Bingo cards for each person (sample given below), pencils*

Purpose: *Learning names, getting to know people better*

Directions:

The object of the game is to get "Bingo," i.e., to fill in people to match the squares in horizontal, vertical or diagonal column. No name may be used more than once in a winning row. The game can be played with all the cards alike, with different facts on each person's card, or with the same facts in different order on the cards. Be creative and make your own cards. It is important when someone shouts "Bingo" to have that person read the names and facts in the winning row.

This game can be made more challenging if people are not allowed to ask questions that require "yes" or "no" answers. If a fact is "loves cats," the person attempting to fill the blank may not ask "Do you like cats?" but will have to ask, "What pets do you love?", etc. Played this way, the game takes a little longer.

B	I	N	G	O
likes history	plays soccer	was in a play	plays piano	middle name is John
ran for office	won a trophy	remembers dreams	sings in the shower	hates pizza
reads mysteries	goes to college	has never been on a train	likes nail polish	uses an electric shaver
was born in fall	likes peanut butter	has been in a foreign country	collects something, e.g., stamps	has never broken a bone
owns a teddy bear	takes dancing lessons	likes to jump rope	saves money	has flown a kite this year

COMMUNITY IS WHERE YOU ARE KNOWN AND LOVED

There is an old saying "A friend is someone who knows you as you are and loves you anyway." Knowing is the beginning of friendship and the reason we stress knowing names. But for community to develop, we must know more about people than their names, and we must be able to demonstrate that we love and support them "anyway." "In community, instead of being ignored, denied, hidden, or changed, human differences are celebrated as gifts."[2]

The following games are designed to lead a group into a slightly deeper knowledge of each other. Many of them can be modified to ask more in-depth questions of a group that has already bonded as a community. Community is something that can never be taken for granted. Because you have established the first step well does not mean it no longer needs attention. Communities are like plants: they need sunshine, food and water to grow. It is easy to rush into the lesson, once a group has become a community, but it will not remain a community without nurturing.

---

2. *Ibid.*, p. 62.

GIFT FIND

---◆---

Group size: Any number

Group age: The ability to read on a second to third grade level is needed for this game. It can be done with an intergenerational group by pairing the young children with adults or teens.

Materials: Lists of gifts (given below), pencils for all

Purpose: Getting to know people better, affirmation

List of gifts:

My best gift is. . . .

1. friendliness_____

2. strength _____

3. neatness_____

4. gentleness _____

5. mechanical ability (fixing things)_____

6. promptness (being on time) _____

7. leadership _____

8. athletics_____

9. coloring_____

10. helpfulness _____

11. singing _____

12. cheerfulness _____

13. schoolwork _____

14. listening_____

15. organization _____

16. playing a musical instrument _____

17. dancing_____

18. carpooling _____

19. creativity _____

20. remembering _____

21. math _____

22. writing _____

23. perseverance (sticking to things) _____

23. being observant (noticing things)_____

24. sensitivity _____

25. honesty_____

It would be helpful for leaders to take careful note of the people in the group and make out these lists of gifts to fit the qualities they have seen. The generic list will work, though.

———————————◆———————————

Directions:

At the start of the game, give people the lists and ask them to read through the qualities, helping younger members with hard words. Ask all members to choose which quality on the list they think is their best quality. Encourage parents to help little ones to decide. At a signal, everyone gets up and moves about, asking other group members their gift. The object of the game is to fill as many of the blank spaces as possible. Two names in the same space does not count. People may not *change* their gift to help out.

The person who fills the most blanks in five minutes wins. You may want to extend the time if it takes the group a little while to warm up.

A variation to this game can be played by having group members choose the people in whom they see a particular gift. Before they can write the name in the blank, though, they must approach the person and explain why they see this person as having a particular gift.

HUNTING FOR COMPLIMENTS

---◆---

Group size: Any size

Group age: This game can be played by anyone old enough to speak, but children between the ages of 8 and 13 are often uncomfortable pointing out good things in others. Little ones will need help writing names and can be paired with an adult.

Materials: Paper and pencil for everyone

Purpose: Affirmation

---◆---

Directions:

This hunt also involves finding good things in others. The object of the game is to sincerely compliment as many people in the group as possible. Each person starts off with a blank sheet of paper and approaches someone in the group and points out a good quality he has noticed in that person. It must be a sincere, *meaningful* compliment, not "I like your shirt!" The complimented person signs her name to the complimenter's list. Little ones can participate by being paired with a parent and they are frequently quite adept at noticing good things in others. Their compliments can be honest and moving.

The leader allows a specified time (10 minutes works well), then calls the game to a halt. The leader checks for the person with the longest list of complimented people. Before she is declared a winner, she must read the name of each person and share with the group the compliment that was given to that person. The group may disqualify any remarks not considered true compliments and declare a new winner.

WHERE DO YOU STAND?

---◆---

Group size: 10-40—*larger if you are working in a large space.*

Group age: *Old enough to understand the statements and walk. The age level will vary with statements used.*

Materials: *An open space to use for a continuum walk, words prepared in advance by the leader, and three signs reading: LOVE, HATE, NO OPINION.*

Purpose: *To review names in a group where people know each other, to understand the members of the group better, to ask people to practice "making a stand" for what they believe*

---◆---

Directions:

Tell the group that you are going to ask them to take a stand on how they feel about certain things. If you stand by the left wall, it means you absolutely love something. (Put the sign LOVE on the wall and demonstrate by standing near it.) If you hate it, you will walk to the right wall. (Put the sign HATE on the right wall.) If you have no preference, stand in the middle. Put the sign NO OPINION on the floor in the middle. Give an example. State "peanut butter" and demonstrate the different places you might stand if you love it, like it, don't care, dislike it, or hate it. Make sure the directions are understood by small children and reassure them that they can ask for help if they get confused. They may have difficulty remembering which wall means which and need to be reminded by whomever is standing near them at the moment. It is important for the group to notice where other people are standing, because when the activity is over, you are going to ask them "Who likes peanut butter?", etc.

Choose several simple things for the continuum. Suggestions: pizza, school, roller coasters, homework, country music, skiing, rock music, baseball, math, chocolate, singing, ice cream, reading, hats, baked beans, spaghetti, merry-go-rounds, television, football, soap operas, talking on the telephone, cookies, mittens, bubbles, science, finger paints, etc. Your choices will depend on the ages of the people in your group. As you read a word, everyone goes to stand in a spot which indicates his feeling about that particular thing. Continue playing for about seven minutes, or until you feel you are losing the group's interest. Ask the group to sit down.

Ask if anyone can tell you someone (other than herself) who loved skiing, who hated peanut butter, who liked science, etc. Little ones will want to tell you that they like or hate the thing you mentioned. Ask them if anyone else in the group was standing with them at that moment because that person feels the same way they do. This helps to keep the game focused, while acknowledging what the young children will want to say. It provides a way to review names, while offering some miscellaneous information about the people in the group.

MAKING A STRONGER STAND

◆

Group size: 10-40, *depending on the size of the space in which the game is played.*

Group age: *Intergenerational; little ones will need help*

Materials: *List of controversial statements prepared in advance by the leader, signs reading: Agree, Disagree, No Opinion*

Purpose: *To invite members to "make a stand," to get to know people's values a little better*

◆

Directions:

This game is played in the same way as the former continuum, but it is for groups who know each other a little better and have developed a rudimentary level of trust. Once again, set up the continuum with AGREE on the left wall, DISAGREE on the right wall, and NO OPINION on the floor in the middle. The group is allowed to talk to each other as they are making their decisions where to stand. (If the group has become fairly relaxed, older ones will try to convince little ones to "come to their side." The leader can encourage this by joining in the game and trying to talk others into joining her in her opinion.)

The reader begins by reading phrases, more value-laden than the words of the earlier game. While these statements are better prepared by a leader who knows her group, some suggestions are given here:

- Adults should be seen and not heard.

- People are at their most creative when they are teens.

- Running is the best way to stay in shape.
- Swimming is the healthiest form of exercise.
- Video stores should not allow children under 17 to rent R-rated videos.
- Children should get an allowance.
- Parents should be responsible for anything their children do.
- People under 16 should be allowed to drive.
- Grandparents make the best babysitters.
- Children should get rewards for good grades.
- There is too much violence on television.
- Grown-ups watch too much television.

Try to fit the statements to the ages and interests in your group. Don't make them too controversial. It is not necessary to do the feedback on names when the game is played this way. The principal point here is to allow people to express their feelings. The game is played the same way as the previous continuum "Make a Stand."

Once you have played this game, as various issues come up in the group, tell everyone you will add them to the continuum list and use the newly compiled list again at a later date.

This game can be used to express feelings about the actions of Biblical characters: "Jacob was wrong to trick Esau." The great value of the walking continuum is that it gives people a chance to practice taking a deliberate stand in the view of others for what they believe in, even if it is only liking baked beans when everyone else hates them. All of us need practice in recognizing we can think very differently from others and still be respected.

PARENT-CHILD FREEZE

━━━━━━━━━━━━━━◆━━━━━━━━━━━━━━

Group age: *Intergenerational*

Group size: *15-40. This can be done in larger groups when all participants are over 10 and able to watch and enjoy when they are not actively involved.*

Materials: *A large adult shoe and a small children's shoe*

Purpose: *To help members understand each other better, to foster parent-child communication*

━━━━━━━━━━━━━━◆━━━━━━━━━━━━━━

Directions:

Ask an adult and child to volunteer for the game. Prepare an argument in advance with the two people chosen to help. Any parent/child issue will do: cleaning your room, staying up late for a TV show, etc., anything a parent and child argue about. Ask the child to assume the parent role (and give the child the large shoe to hold), and the parent the child role (and the small shoe). Tell the group that they are about to eavesdrop on a parent/child argument. They will know which person is being the parent in the argument because the parent will be the person holding the big shoe, the child will hold the little one. Move the two people who have been prepared to the center of the group. Let them begin to argue. Once all understand what the argument is about and who is playing which part (ask the group to allow at least two minutes), any person in the group can call FREEZE, go to the center and take either shoe, and continue the argument from the adult perspective, if they have taken the large shoe, or from the child's perspective, if they have taken the small one. It takes a group a few minutes to want to participate in this activity, but then the problem becomes giving each person who jumps in enough time to do or say something. Encourage people, if they can, to take the role they do NOT have in the family.

Once this game is learned as an icebreaker, it can later be used in discussions of moral issues that are impacting the life of the group. As it becomes more familiar, children and adults will introduce topics into the argument that they have been afraid to discuss at home. It is important to remain nonjudgmental and to keep the tone light. This is not group therapy; it is a tool to enable discussion.

STATUES

◆

Group size: 5-10 families. (This activity is specifically for families. It can be done in large groups, but it becomes time consuming.)

Group age: Intergenerational

Materials: None

Purpose: To help families understand themselves better and to share who they are with the group.

◆

Directions:

Ask the group if any of them have seen the statue "The Thinker" by Rodin. Someone in the group probably has. Ask that person to demonstrate how the statue is posed. If no one in the group knows, demonstrate yourself, sitting with knees slightly spread apart, elbow on knee, chin resting on the hand. The person in the statue really looks like he is thinking. It is possible, in a statue, to capture an action like thinking or a quality like thoughtfulness.

Ask each family to come up with what they feel is their outstanding *positive* trait. It is important to stress the positive part. Ask the family to figure out a way to create a statue, using their own bodies, that will demonstrate that trait. Give the families some separate space to work in (it doesn't need to be a separate room, just a little area) and allow 5-10 minutes (depending on how quickly they appear to be accomplishing the task.) This activity moves more quickly with families with only young children since the adults do not have to discuss and tend to take control. Move among the families and make sure the children are being heard. Singles in a group can create their own statues or help leaders.

Bring the families back and allow them, one at a time, to share their statues. The group can guess the outstanding trait they are trying to demonstrate.

This activity can be modified to express actions that the family enjoys doing together, like roasting marshmallows around a campfire, or things they do together but dislike, like laundry or yard work.

WHERE ARE YOU?

---◆---

Group size: 10-25 people

Group age: Teen to adult

Materials: A writing surface, such as a chalk board or easel, and chalk or marker

Purpose: To become more present to the group and the activity at hand

---◆---

Directions:

Begin by writing on the surface the percentage of yourself that is actually present to the group. Explain. It may be that only 60% of you is present because 20% of you is still at the office, 5% with the soccer game you didn't get to see, 10% with the homework you were trying to help your son do, and 5% of you is just missing. It got mislaid in the rush to get to the meeting. Invite others to share by writing their percentage on the board.

This can be a long warm-up because people often have several things to say. Encourage them to be brief. Enumerating the things often helps us to let go of them and be truly present. This is especially good for meetings where only the adults may be present.

The game can be played more simply (to include younger children) by asking which part of your body is here and which part is not and why. The heart may be in the meeting, but the head may be back with the math assignment.

THE ORCHESTRA

---◆---

Group size: *10-35—(too many people can make this unwieldy)*

Group age: *Intergenerational*

Materials: *Pencil and paper for each family, names of each family in the group on separate sheets of paper.*

Purpose: *Affirmation*

---◆---

Directions:

Put the slips of paper with the family names in a dish. Instruct the families that they will be working together as a family for this activity. Single-person households need to work alone for this activity.

Each family (household) draws a slip of paper from the dish. If they draw their own name, they should put it back and draw again. The family is to consider the family they have drawn. If the group were an orchestra, what instrument would each member of that family be playing, and why?

Give people enough time to assign instruments, then call them back to the group. The game can be made more interesting for little ones by having pictures of instruments, drawn or cut from catalogs, to put people's names on. Let one family at a time present to the family they drew the instruments they see them as being. They should say each person's name and explain why that person is the violin, piano, etc., for the group.

This activity really needs to end with a song. In groups with many small children, everyone can be encouraged to "play" their instrument for the song. (Middle-schoolers will absolutely refuse to do anything that corny.)

It Feels Like a Gift

---◆---

Group size: 10-25—*too many more people would take too long.*

Group age: *Intergenerational, but small children will need help.*

Materials: *"It feels like a gift" cards, enough for every person, samples given here.*

Purpose: *To recognize the everyday gifts we give to one another*

Sample cards:

Helping feels like a gift when. . . .

Listening feels like a gift when . . .

A visit feels like a gift when . . .

A phone call feels like a gift when . . .

A loan feels like a gift when . . .

Flowers feel like a gift when . . .

An invitation feels like a gift when . . .

Forgiveness feels like a gift when . . .

Sharing feels like a gift when . . .

Caring feels like a gift when . . .

Friendship feels like a gift when . . .

A letter feels like a gift when . . .

A compliment feels like a gift when . . .

A photograph feels like a gift when . . .

A meal feels like a gift when . . .

A friend feels like a gift when . . .

Acceptance feels like a gift when . . .

A smile feels like a gift when . . .

A touch feels like a gift when . . .
Tears feel like a gift when . . .
Rain feels like a gift when . . .
Sunshine feels like a gift when . . .

———————————◆———————————

Directions:

The object of this game is to help the community to understand that all gifts don't come in packages with pretty wrappings. Some of the best gifts are the ones we give each other every day.

Ask each person in the group to take a card and think about a time when someone gave them the gift written on it, or when they gave the gift to someone. The more specific they can be, the better. For example, "A compliment feels like a gift when I've studied real hard for a test and the teacher says it shows, like yesterday in math." Young children will need a parent or others to read their cards to them and to help them choose situations. Don't be afraid to let them share. They are often more capable of recognizing the gift in the ordinary.

A COMMUNITY WORKS TOGETHER

An important part of being community is the ability to work together. It isn't enough to know one another's names and to care about each other. We also need to be able to look outward together, to care together about something beyond us.

Intergenerational communities take the longest of any form of community to learn to work together. Adults frequently begin by believing they are only "there for the kids," pushing the children forward in each situation, whispering suggestions in their ears, instead of volunteering themselves. Once the adults get caught up in the situation, though, they run the risk of taking over. How many boxcar derbies have we seen with cars built by adult men screaming at each other while bewildered Cub Scouts stood by, or 4-H fashion shows with clothes clearly made by mothers! (My comparisons here are sexist; unfortunately, they reflect the reality of many of these events.) Adults have little experience of working with children outside of home situations, and the home and yard cleaning and repair that once provided that opportunity is fast disappearing.

These games are an attempt to offer adults and children fun ways to work together. There may be problems to be solved, races to be won, etc. The competition is not the key here. The important issue is the cooperation.

Groups of like ages also benefit from games that prepare them for more serious work together. The game helps develop a cooperation mind-set before the work actually begins. Frequently, what is most needed in a group is the simple ability to have fun together. *Remember to take Time to Play.*

Hidden Treasure

◆

Group size: *12-32 people in four teams. The game can accommodate more people by breaking into more teams, but eight on a team is the real limit for having everyone involved.*

Group ages: *Intergenerational*

Materials: *Paper bag for each team, lists of hidden treasures (sample given below)*

Purpose: *Learning to function as a team*

Sample list:

fork	ashtray	picture	pencil
glasses	sweater	sneaker	whistle
blush	sheet music	Bible	candle
license	stopwatch	checkbook	ticket stub
scarf	envelope	battery	lollipop
cough drop	pen	eraser	souvenir
flower	1944 penny	trophy	newspaper
lipstick	marbles	acorn	matches

◆

Directions:

The leader needs to prepare by deciding how many teams will be needed and making a list for each team. The lists can be the same or different, but should be equally difficult. The list given here is simply a sample, and longer than your lists need to be. Choose things you know have a chance of being available in the area, on people, in purses, pockets, etc.

Divide the group into teams and let them discuss the list. Decide how much time will be allowed—the more people on a team, the less time they should be given. Do not allow enough time for any team to find all the articles. If you want to use the game as a simple warm-up, make the lists short, but not so short any team will find everything. When the command is given, everyone scrambles to find the articles.

All members of the team will need to work together. If you are working with families, split them up. This adds to the fun, since children will go to their parents on other teams to try to con them out of articles they know they are carrying. If you decide to divide the groups up by age, be careful about your choice of articles, since children would be disadvantaged by many of the articles on the sample list given.

The winning team is the one that comes up with the greatest number of *legitimate* articles. Allow time in your planning for people to share the articles they have found, since some are likely to be quite creative.

Bumps on a Log

---◆---

Group size: 10-16, or teams of 10-16 people

Group age: Intergenerational

Materials: A log for each team, long enough to support the number of people on the team. A 2x4 or 2x6 (if you want it to be easier) can take the place of the log. This game needs to be played in a large room with a floor that can support these logs, or played outside.

Purpose: Reviewing names, working together

---◆---

Directions:

If you have more than 16 people in your group, split into teams. It is important to have at least eight people on a team for the game to be fun. Show each team their "log" and invite them to go and stand on it.

Once all members are standing on the log, ask them to get into alphabetical order by first names, without ever stepping off the log! The idea is for every team to succeed in doing this, not to compete to do it first. Little ones can crawl under people's legs and are very handy to have on your log. They will need to be reminded to stay on the log, (but it does not count if they forget). Once a group has completed the task, they should sound off, people shouting their names in order. The group is free to decide which end of the log will be the "A" and which end the "Z".

This game can be played again at a later date by changing the ordering. Once people see the logs again, they will make sure they get on them alphabetically. Try having them arrange themselves by birthdates, with January as the starting point. Last names can also work, if you are not dealing with families.

Supporting the Group

---◆---

Group size: Any size divided into teams of 8-10 people
Group age: Intergenerational
Materials: A telephone book for each team
Purpose: Group problem-solving

---◆---

Directions:

Give each group a telephone book and a space to work where they will not be in the direct line of vision of the other groups. Instruct the groups:

"The object of this activity is to have everyone in the group supported by the telephone book (just as we are all supported by the Bible). Arrange yourselves in such a way that everyone in the group is supported by one foot on the book. The other foot *may not* be touching the floor."

How you word your directions is important. By not instructing the group to "stand on" the book, some may find other, creative ways of doing the exercise. Tell the groups to come back and sit down as soon as they are ready to demonstrate to others how they have solved the problem. Do not give them more than 5-7 minutes. Have everyone demonstrate the group's solutions.

BEING FIRST ISN'T ALWAYS WINNING

---◆---

This is an OUTSIDE game.

Group size: *Any size*

Group age: *Intergenerational. This game works best with people of very different ages and sizes.*

Materials: *Several pieces of rope, one for every two people in the group.*

Purpose: *Cooperation*

---◆---

Directions:

This is a race that is not what it appears to be. Mark an area outside as the starting and finish line. If the course meanders at all, mark that. This is best played on a grassy surface so that no one gets hurt.

Begin by choosing two judges. They can be asked in advance and should be people in the group who may not be comfortable running, or may not be able to run. If you have several people in this category, place them at strategic points along the track. Tell your judges *only* that they will be judging *not* who runs the fastest, but who works together the best. This may be the fastest couple, but it may not.

Pair everyone else off. You may want to choose pairs or allow them to choose their own. Ask tall people to team up with small ones, since they will need help. The judges should be watching the early stages for signs of cooperation.

Once everyone has a partner, instruct the partners to tie their legs together at the ankles (three-legged race style) and line up at the starting line. When you give the signal, they are to run as fast and as *carefully* as they can to the finish. Tell the group that the most important thing is to work with your partner. Some may hear this and catch on, others will just want to race.

Run the race. At the end of the race, tell everyone the judges are going to convene to decide the winners. Give the judges a few minutes, then let them pronounce the "winners" with an explanation of why they won. There can be as many winners as there are people really trying to work together. You may want to name first, second, and third places.

Competition is not necessarily bad. It becomes bad when our total focus is on beating others. We can win by cooperation, and sometimes that even wins the race.

HUMAN KNOT

◆

Group size: *10-20, or teams of 10 to 20*

Group age: *This game is difficult to play with people who vary too much in size. While it is something children over three can understand and do, you may want to put them in a separate group from the 12+ because the size difference will be difficult.*

Materials: *None*

Purpose: *Working together, reviewing names*

◆

Directions:

Invite the group to stand in a circle facing the center, or in two circles to accommodate very different sizes or large numbers. Everyone joins hands. The leader begins by saying "My right hand is holding N . . .'s left hand." Each person in the group states whose left hand is in his right hand and carefully remembers this person. If there is more than one group, do this announcing separately, not simultaneously. Instruct everyone to drop hands and have people take different positions in the circle, *without* joining hands. *Remaining in their new positions,* members take the *same* left hand that was *originally* in their right hands. This will involve reaching across the group, etc., and all hands should be joined when everyone has done this. Without letting go of any hands, the group must try to untangle itself.

MUSICAL CHAIRS

◆

Group size: 10-20. *This will not work with a very large group. If your group is larger, you may want to divide them into teams and have one team watch the other play.*

Group age: 3-adult

Materials: *Roughly enough chairs for everyone to sit—it will not affect the game if you are missing a few.*

Purpose: *Learning to work together as a group*

◆

Directions:

In *Maybe, Maybe Not,* Robert Fulghum offers a unique way to play musical chairs. First, he suggests playing it in the traditional way we all learned as children, but removing *several* chairs every time the music stops to keep the game moving. After someone has claimed the last chair, discuss how everyone feels about the game.

Next, tell everyone the object of the game will be for *everyone* to find a place to sit down every time the music stops. Remove only a couple of chairs the first time the music stops. People will decide to scramble for laps, etc. Each time remove a few more chairs until everyone is attempting to sit on one chair. Ask the group to consider why this game feels different from the first way it was played. The group will probably discover that including others is always more fun than excluding them. This is an excellent game for a night that deals with church or community.

SANDMAN

◆

Group size: 10+. *The only limit on the size of the group is that everyone must be able to have visual contact with everyone else.*

Group age: Intergenerational

Materials: None

Purpose: Fun

◆

Directions:

Tell the group the Sandman is coming to put them to sleep. No one knows who the Sandman is, but she will put you to sleep by winking at you. The idea is to catch the Sandman before she catches you. If you look at the Sandman and she winks at you, you must instantly put your head down and keep it there until the game is over. But if you see someone wink at another person and his head goes down, you may accuse the winker of being the Sandman.

Prepare someone in advance to play the Sandman and warn that person not to tell anyone. Explain the directions carefully to the group, showing the children how the Sandman might wink at them. Don't be too concerned if they get "put to sleep" and don't respond. Once somebody guesses the Sandman, the game is over. If you want to have a second round, go around the group and whisper in each person's ear "You are not the Sandman." In one person's ear whisper "You are the Sandman." Play again.

This is a purely-for-fun game, but it can be helpful encouraging children to make eye contact with others.

BUTTON, BUTTON, WHO'S GOT THE BUTTON?

Group size: Any size

Group age: Works best with young children or family groups with many young children

Materials: A button. In choosing a button, keep in mind the size of the hands of the younger people who will be playing.

Purpose: Fun

Directions:

This is an old birthday party game. Have everyone sit in a circle and hold out both hands, palms pressed together, as if in prayer, fingers pointed straight out. The leader says that he has a button and he will go around the group and give it to someone. You must watch carefully to discover who has the button, but don't say anything until you are asked.

The leader presses his hands together in the same praying manner, only with a button in the palms. He goes around the circle, pushing his hands through each of the outstretched pairs of hands. It is important to demonstrate how to do this to the group, so that young people will keep the bottom of their palms pressed together while the leader's hands are in theirs. The leader tries to make it look as if he is dropping the button into each person's hands. Everyone must be warned to keep their hands pressed tightly together so they will not reveal whether or not they have the button.

The button is eventually dropped into one person's hands and the leader continues on around the group. Then he asks the group to tell him who has the button. Members must raise their hands, palms still pressed together. The first person to guess correctly becomes the "button person" and the game is played again.

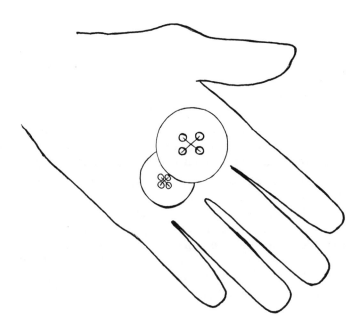

More Statues

$\blacklozenge$

Group size: Teams of 6 to 10 people
Group age: Intergenerational
Materials: None
Purpose: Working together

$\blacklozenge$

Directions:

Divide the group into subgroups of 6-10 people. If you are working with an intergenerational group, make sure there is a mixture of ages in each group, since this would be too abstract a task for a group of little ones. The leader must choose in advance what the group will be "statueing." Ideas that work well: church, family, school, community, the particular community in which you are doing the exercise.

Each group will be given the same topic, e.g., church. Ask the groups to make a statue (it is allowed to have moving parts) that demonstrates what they think church is or how they feel about it. Give all the groups about 10 minutes to work, then ask them to share their statues with everyone else. Let the rest of the group guess what the parts of the statue mean. If it needs explanation, the statue group can explain, or change the statue to demonstrate better.

New Life Scavenger Hunt

◆

This is an OUTSIDE, SPRINGTIME game.

Group size: Any size, divided into groups of 6-8

Group age: Intergenerational, little ones with parents

Materials: Paper bags for each group

Purpose: Working together

◆

Directions:

(Note: This game will not work in the city, except in a park.)

Divide your group into teams of similar size, mixing ages up but keeping small ones with parents for their own safety. Tell the groups they are to go outside and find signs of new life. They do not all have to be traditional signs, like seeds. The group may want to bring something and argue that it is a sign of new life. The group as a whole will decide whether or not the sign is legitimate.

This game takes a little longer than most. Tell the groups they have 15 minutes, and make sure someone in the group has a watch. They will have one item they have found deducted for every minute they are late. (A penalty is important to prevent people from simply wandering off for the evening!)

Teams return with items they have found and explain why each is a sign of new life. The group as a whole can eliminate any articles they feel are not legitimate signs of life. One item is deducted for every minute a team is late. The team with the largest number of true "signs of new life" wins.

WHO AM I?

◆

Group size: Any size

Group age: Intergenerational

Materials: Straight pins, slips of paper with the name of a biblical character written on each, enough so that each person in the group will have one, sample characters given below

Purpose: Working together

Sample list of characters:

Adam	Eve	Cain	Abel	Noah
Abraham	Isaac	Jacob	Esau	Leah
Rachel	Rebecca	Joseph	Judah	Benjamin
Saul	David	Solomon	Isaiah	Jeremiah
Ruth	Deborah	Samson	Mary	Jesus
Elizabeth	Simon Peter	John the Baptist	Joseph	Andrew
James	John	Paul	Matthew	Herod
Pilate	Nicodemus	Anna	Judas	

◆

Directions:

Write the name of a biblical character on each slip of paper, focusing on characters that have been part of the learning experience this year. As members enter, a name is pinned on their backs. The names of easy characters, such as Mary, Joseph, Jesus, Adam, Eve, Noah, and Abraham should be saved for the young children, while adults are given the most difficult names.

Once everyone has arrived, explain to the group that they must discover who they are. They are allowed to ask each person in the community one question that can be answered in one word, e.g., "What kind of job did I have?" "Fisherman." When they think they know who they are, members can go sit down. Young children are not bound by the one-word-answer rule and should be given big hints: e.g., "You were killed by your brother, Cain." When everyone (or almost everyone) is seated, ask each person who he thinks he is and why. Then have each stand up and turn around. If they are right, applaud and take the slip of paper off. If they are not right, someone in the group should help them out, e.g., "You are right thinking you are Peter because he was a fisherman, but this fisherman never became the head of the Church, even though he met Jesus before his brother, Peter." Hints should be broad and easy, at this point. As soon as someone guesses who she is, everyone should applaud. If there are people who have not yet guessed who they are, they should stand with their backs to the group while people give them hints. Explain to the group that some of the characters are far more difficult and lesser known than others, if they don't see this readily. As people guess who they are, have them sit down.

This game takes a little longer than the other icebreakers but it can be an excellent review for a group that has been studying Scripture.

BIBLICAL TIME LINE

---◆---

Group size: Any size

Group age: Intergenerational

Materials: Index cards with a historical biblical character on each, Bibles

Purpose: Review

---◆---

Directions:

On entering the home or group, each person is given a card with a name on it. When everyone is present, ask the group to arrange themselves in chronological order, beginning with Adam and Eve. Bibles can be used, and people are free to ask one another for help. Easy characters should be given to younger children.

This can be a great way to get people in line for a pot-luck supper, or any social event that requires taking turns. It also provides a way to review Bible characters and their place in history.

CIRCLE GAMES

If the majority of children in your group are preschoolers, old-fashioned circle games are wonderful icebreakers and can be used throughout a gathering. Young children have much shorter attention spans, and it does not hurt a lesson to break for 10 minutes in the middle for a game.

In selecting games, be careful about using ones such as *Farmer in the Dell*, where an arbitrary selection process takes place and some children may be left out. Games that work well: *a Tisket, a Tasket, Little Sally Saucer, Bluebird, Butcher Shop, London Bridge*, or any that give everyone an equal opportunity to join in. Local libraries should have copies of words and music for most of these games. Circle games have existed for over 2,000 years. We should not underestimate their importance in the development of a child or a community.

SIMON SAYS

Simon Says is another one of those games that can be pulled out when your mind is blank and you have no icebreaker for the evening. Doing the *Hokey Pokey* is fun with a group that is not too inhibited. Check out some of the games from your childhood, from Scouts and 4-H and other group activities. You'll find many that can be modified for community and classroom.

2

RITUALS

A Community Shares
Symbols and Prayer

"Rituals are expressions of values and attitudes in the form of symbolic action."[3] Communities develop rituals for gathering and separating, for celebrating and for mourning, for forgiving and being forgiven. Through the ritual, a society not only acts out the sacred meaning symbolized in the action, it reminds its members to enter into the meaning. "The unity of a group, like all its cultural values, must find symbolic expression. . . . The symbol is at once a definite focus of interest, a means of communication, and a common ground of understanding."[4]

Every small community needs to develop rituals that help to identify the importance and meaning of the community for the members themselves. The beginning of this "symbolic action" lies in the use of symbol.

The root of "symbol" is the Greek word *symbollein,* "to match," and refers to an ancient custom. When an agreement was reached or a contract made in ancient Greece, it was customary to break something in two: a piece of pottery, a ring, a tablet. Each of the parties to the agreement was given one of the pieces or *symbol.* Either party could lay claim to their part of the agreement by presenting the *symbol* and connecting it to the other piece of the object. The word eventually came to mean "recognition sign," e.g., the fish was a symbol by which the early Christians recognized one another.

---

3. Joseph Martos, *Doors to the Sacred* (Garden City, NY: Doubleday, 1982) p. 26.

4. F.W. Dillistone. *The Power of Symbol in Religion and Culture* (New York: Crossroads, 1986).

Symbols became ways in which we understood ourselves and made that meaning known to others. Symbols are more than just signs, since they point to a meaning that is often beyond the power of words to express. Toynbee pointed out that a symbol does not reproduce that which it represents, it illuminates. It is an instrument to extend our vision, stimulate imagination and deepen our understanding.

Symbolic action is vital to any group working toward community. The first symbolic act of a group was discussed earlier and involved naming the group (p. 6). A concrete symbol needs to be found that expresses the meaning of the name on a deeper level than words. A carefully chosen symbol is capable of carrying, not only the value we assign it, but its own value and its own power to move us.

One intergenerational group named itself "Circles of Love," and chose as its symbol a set of wooden concentric circles, with each household represented by one of the circles. When the symbol was put together at the beginning of a meeting, it was intended to be instantly obvious if anyone was missing. The circle symbol also conveyed all the ancient meanings of "completeness," "no beginning or end," etc., that the circle has always represented, but the wooden symbol itself made other things obvious. Cut with a jigsaw, the circles were not completely smooth and did not fit together easily, symbolic of the struggles the group faced as they worked toward community. In decorating the circles, several people had chosen to wrap ribbon around the outside of the wood, covering the circle and making the fit impossible. (Covering up, hiding true identity also works against community.) The circles had developed a message of their own, and as the group struggled to put them together each week, sanding down rough edges, they reminded the members of all they were called to be for one another.

Good symbols need to be more than clever ideas. The symbols that have the best chance of enduring are those rooted in some of our ancient symbols, such as water, rainbows, wind. These symbols have maintained for centuries a meaning beyond their simple, concrete definitions. They possess the power to become the focal point of a group and a means by which the group can interpret its own actions. In struggling to find symbols for your group, keep in mind how the group understands itself, what ancient symbols are common to their understanding and their culture, the group's vision for itself and how the symbol will relate to that vision.

The following symbols have been adapted and used in youth groups, intergenerational groups, and FIRE groups with varying degrees of success. They are offered here not to be reproduced, but to jumpstart your own symbolic thinking and provide vehicles for the ritual actions that will be discussed later. In creating your symbol, make it beautiful and durable and deserving of respect.

RAINBOW: A rainbow can be made with an arc for each family. A center semi-circle allows for an eighth household, or a piece to represent the Church, the base on which we rest. Rainbows are a sign of covenant and hope.
(Ritual p. 94)

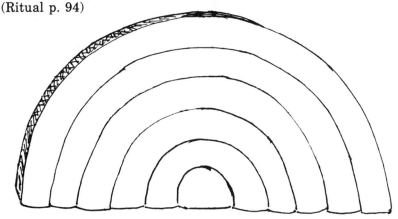

CONCENTRIC CIRCLES:
Concentric circles can be carved out of wood or cut out of heavy cardboard and given to families to decorate. The circle is a sign of eternity, of connection, of equality, of reality that never ends.
(Ritual p. 100)

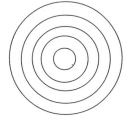

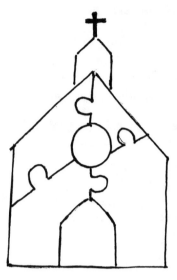

CHURCH: A church can be made out of wood or heavy cardboard and cut into puzzle pieces, with a piece for each family, or members, and one piece to represent the rest of the community. The members decorate their piece. A small cross or crucifix for the top of the steeple can be carried home by the family member that will host the next meeting, or the member that will lead prayer, or the leader, or a designated "cross-bearer."
(No specific ritual is given, but p. 98 can be used effectively)

STAR: A five-pointed star, or star of David, carved out of wood or heavy cardboard, with a diamond for each family member. A five-pronged star can be made with a central circle. The star has represented a "way to Jesus" since the first Epiphany, as well as a guiding light to all navigators. (Ritual p. 103)

CROSSES: One of the most basic symbols of Christianity, crosses can be constructed in many ways. The beams of a wooden cross can represent the families/members and fit together, puzzle-style, when the families are assembled. A cross can be made from narrow logs, halved to lie flat, with hollows carved out for candles. Each family or member is given a candle to light up the cross. Square crosses can be constructed to fit together in a pattern that always seems incomplete and longs for more crosses. Crosses can be made of wood and decorated by families/members. (Ritual p. 98)

FIRE: A central candle can be placed in a base that allows a candle for each family or member to be mounted around it. The opening ritual will include taking light from the central candle to light the individual ones. Sharing the light can also be demonstrated by using different-colored candles for the families/members and a central, large white one for the group. At the end of each meeting, families/members allow a little of the colored wax from their candles to drip onto the white one, as part of their closing prayer. Eventually, the

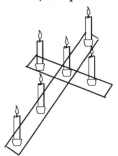

"group" candle will be transformed. Small votive candles can also be used for each family, or member, and the light can be carefully carried in them from home (or at least from outside the meeting place) into the meeting, since we also bring the light with us as well as receive it. (Ritual p. 92)

WATER: A central, clear receptacle, with a spout for pouring, is needed to represent the group. Each family or member has a small vial for carrying water, something worthy to carry a symbol of life, not an old pill or soda bottle. Each member brings its water to the meeting and adds it to the receptacle. The group vase is only full when all the families\members are present. As they leave, members take water back from the vase; only now it as been changed by mingling with the group. Water from the groups can be taken to large group celebrations at church, where it is blessed and the same process takes place. (Ritual p. 87)

SHIP: A ship can be made with masts for each family or member. The ship is a symbol of voyage; we depend on one another to help us catch the wind in our sails. (Ritual p. 90)

WIND CHIMES: Wind chimes can be made from kits of shells created for that purpose. Each family is given a string of shells, one shell for each family member, which can be painted or decorated. A central circle represents the group, and the shells are hung from it each time the group gathers. The shells catch the music in the wind. The wind has been an accepted symbol of life and Spirit since early Hebrew Testament times. (Ritual p. 90)

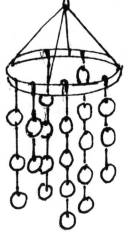

KITE: A group can make and decorate a kite, perhaps use it for their covenant. Each family or member is given a "bow" to decorate for the tail. The kite reminds us again of the wind, the power of the spirit in our lives, while the tail reminds us of the balance we offer to each other. (Ritual p. 90)

SUNDIAL: A sundial can be constructed of wood or heavy card-board in pieces that can be covered with foil mottled to look like weathered metal, and given to each

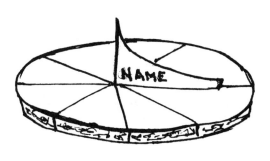

family or member. Sundials remind us not only of the significance of time, but the significance of shadows in helping us to understand the "time" in our life. Sundials remind us where the sun is when all we can see are shadows. (Ritual p. 96)

MINUTE TIMERS: Egg timers and one-minute timers are available from most kitchen supply stores. They can be brought to each meeting as a symbol of the time we are willing to give to God and to each other. (Ritual p. 96)

A Community Celebrates Ritual

"Ritual is the means by which collective beliefs and ideals are simultaneously generated, experienced, and affirmed as real by the community."[5] Aidan Cavanaugh calls it the way we review and renew what we believe.

Ritual offers us the opportunity to pray in a comfortable, known fashion. Just as practice exercises on the piano strengthen specific fingers and muscles by repetition, ritual is the opportunity to "practice" praying, a familiar gateway to a prayerful mindset. Its very familiarity is part of its great value. And just as the piano exercises can be beautiful music (check out J.S. Bach), so simple rituals can also comprise beautiful prayer.

The following rituals are offered with this in mind. They follow the same general format, and the same ritual can be used repeatedly by a group. The first set offer the opportunity to celebrate specific times, places and ideas with ritual; the second set are created around the symbols suggested on the previous pages for group use. All of the rituals can be used by any group simply by using the adaptations recommended in each "preparation" section. Directions for assembling a group symbol are included in *italics* wherever this is appropriate. A simple closing given with many of the rituals offers the opportunity to send households or individuals home at the end of the meeting with their piece of the symbol.

All of the rituals are designed as simple introductions to group meetings or classes. They can be developed into longer rituals that stand alone by using the possible readings included at the end of each ritual and by closing with the Lord's Prayer and song.

---

5. Emile Durkeim. *The Elementary Forms of Religious Life*. trans. J.W. Swain (New York: Free Press, 1965) p. 51.

Questioning

Preparation

Instruct each person to choose a question from Scripture. A list of possible questions is included here, but encourage people to look for their own. Ask families to help little ones by reading several questions and talking about their possible meanings. Once each person in the household has chosen a question, ask him/her to choose one that represents the feelings of the family as a whole. It may be one of the ones an individual chose, or a totally different question.

List of Possible Questions:

- Am I my brother's keeper? (Gen. 4:9)
- I lift my eyes to the mountains; from where shall come my help? (Ps. 121:1)
- Where can I hide from your Spirit? (Ps. 139:7)
- Who do you say that I am? (Matt. 16:14)
- Who are you, Lord? (Acts 9:5)
- What sign will you give to show us that we should believe in you? (John 6:30)
- How can a grown person be born again? Can we go back into our mother's womb and be born again? (John 3:4-5)
- Are you "He who is to come" or do we look for another? (Matt. 11:4)
- Is it lawful to work a cure on the Sabbath? (Matt. 12:10)
- What is truth? (John 18:38)
- Who is the greatest in the kingdom of heaven? (Matt. 18:1)

- What about us? . . . We have left everything and followed you. (Mark 10:28)
- How can anyone give this people sufficient bread? (Mark 8:4)
- Have (we) eyes, but no sight; ears but no hearing? (Mark 17:18)
- Good Teacher, what must I do to have everlasting life? (Mark 10:17)
- What do you want me to do for you? (Matt. 20:32)
- How long will you hide your face from me? (Ps. 13:2)
- How can this be? (Luke 1:34)

Parents may want to help children remember their quote by writing out the question and letting them carry it to the meeting.

Ritual

Opening Song:

Choose any song that focuses on searching, on our uncertainty.

Leader: We are so uncertain, God.

We long for answers.

We want to be sure.

Sure that we have followed the right path,

Certain we have spoken the right words,

Studied the right chapters,

Chosen the right friends.

Help us to remember that You are mystery,

Life is mystery.

Help us to live with the questions.

In groups using symbol as an expression of unity, households come forward, one at a time, add their piece of the symbol, and speak their *family question.*

(Allow the group to sit quietly for a few moments, then the leader voices her question aloud. Other people speak up randomly until all questions have been shared.)

Leader: Help us to remember, Lord, that You are mystery.

Help us to live with the questions,

One day at a time,

One word at a time.

You commanded us to ask for our needs, and so I invite each of us to voice our special intentions. We will respond, **"Hear us, O Lord."**

(Spontaneous prayer of the faithful)

Leader: We ask that you hear us, Lord, and answer our needs. We ask this in the name of Jesus.

(Depending on what is to follow, you may want to repeat your opening song, a group theme song, or move directly to the next part of the meeting.)

Closing

Leader: Questions are starting points,

Beginnings of new journeys,

Windows

To insight

And deeper faith.

Invite each of the families/households to come forward and take their piece of the symbol, while saying: **"Lord, keep our family open to all the questions in our lives."**

Because the questions themselves are Scripture, no additional readings are given for this ritual.

Bread

Preparation

The leader should prepare a centerpiece around the theme of bread, with a special plate holding an unconsecrated host in the center. Ask each family/household or individual to bring a particular type of bread to the meeting. It is okay to buy the bread, but better not to have it sliced and packaged. Assign different types of bread to different families or individuals. You will need whole wheat or a basic yeast bread, soda bread, unleavened bread (such as matza), crackers, gingerbread. Ask everyone to bring the bread in a low basket with a linen napkin. Ask the family/household to designate someone who will hold it aloft while the prayer over it is being spoken, then add it to the centerpiece of bread.

Ritual

Opening Song:

"I Am the Bread of Life," or any song that focuses on bread-of-life themes.

Reader 1: "I am the bread of life. Whoever comes to me will never be hungry; and those who believe in me will never thirst." John 6:35

Reader 2: Lord, (Basic bread held up by member)
We, too, are bread
For the life of the world.
But there are many kinds of bread,
As there are many people.
There is the ordinary

Yeast (whole wheat) bread,
Breads that have been given ample time and
warmth
  For the yeast to grow,
  Families favored
  With stable homes,
  Enough to eat.
  May we use their gifts
  To nourish the world.

*　　*　　*

(soda bread held aloft by member)

There is soda bread,
  Quick bread;
  Those who are in need,
  Who have no time to wait
  For yeast to rise.
  Our bread has raisins,
  For though they are wanting
  They are still gifted
  And still deserving
  Of the good things of the earth.
  May we remember their need
  As we nourish the earth.

*　　*　　*

(unleavened bread raised)
Unleavened bread
  Is for those
  Who have been flattened
  By oppression and injustice.
  Let our hunger for bread.
  Teach us to hunger and thirst
  For justice.

*   *   *

(crackers raised)

Crackers

> Represent the elderly,
> Salty with wisdom,
> Fragile with age.
> Let this bread
> Teach us to value wisdom,
> To treat it gently
> When it has grown fragile.

*   *   *

(Gingerbread raised)

Gingerbread,

> Spicy bread,
> For all those
> Who do more than nourish,
> Who bring spice to our lives.

*   *   *

(Leader raises unconsecrated host.)

Leader: "Blessed are you, Lord, God of all creation. Through your goodness we have this bread to offer, which earth has given and human hands have made. It will become for us the bread of life."

Leader: Think for a moment of the people who have been bread in your life. We will pass each loaf of bread. Break a piece and pray for someone you have known who has been gingerbread, whole wheat bread, etc.

(Play quiet music until everyone has had a chance to have a small piece of each bread.)

Leader: Help us to remember, Lord, we are called to be bread for the world. We ask this in the name of Jesus.

All: Amen

Beauty of Autumn

(For areas where leaves change color)

Preparation

Ask each family or household to go for a walk. Each person is to find a leaf which, for some reason, reminds her of herself, then prepare a one-line prayer, thanking God for the particular trait that she and the leaf share, e.g., "Thank you, God, for making me solid and dependable like the stem of the hickory leaf.

Ritual

Opening Song:

Any song that deals with the beauty of creation, any thanksgiving song.

Reader 1: "We are God's work of art, created in Christ Jesus to live the good life as from the beginning he meant us to live it." Ephesians 2:10

Reader 2: God, our God,

You have painted our world.

Had You given us

Just one maple,

One tree that changed

Magnificently with the seasons,

We would have been in awe.

We would have fenced it round,

Named it

One of the seven wonders of the world,

69

And planned to visit
At least once in our lifetime.
But You lavish us with beauty
And, glutted,
We risk walking unseeing
Through Your world.
Open our eyes
To the beauty of our world
And each other.

Leader: (Placing the leaf in a vase and placing first piece of family symbol) "Thank you, God, for making me. . . ."

Other individuals follow, families or households placing their symbol as each person from that household comes forward with a leaf.)

Leader: Loving God, the earth is beautiful in its dying. Let it remind us of the power pain and death have to make us beautiful. We ask this in the name of Jesus.

All: Amen.

Possible Readings:

Ephesians 2:1-10, Isaiah 43:1-2

Beginning of the School Year

Preparation

Have each person bring a symbol of school opening. Make a small centerpiece of books, pencils, calculator and candle, with space for group members to add their own symbols *and to assemble the group symbol.* Parents may want to bring symbols of making lunches or carpooling; singles may be taking a course, or bring a symbol of driving more carefully or leaving earlier to allow for school buses.

Ritual

Opening Song:

Since it is likely that this will be your first meeting of the year, simply choose an upbeat, gathering song.

Reader 1: "Now, Lord, give me wisdom and knowledge."
2 Chr 1:12

Reader 2: Learning,

For some of us, so easy,

So filled with rewards,

For others, so difficult,

So filled with frustration.

Help us, God, to be patient

With our own limits

And with the limits of others,

To give one another

The space and time

Each needs to grow.

(The leader explains that he will call each family forward with a prayer for them, and they can add their school symbol to the centerpiece. As they come forward, they may voice any specific prayers they have, and the group will respond, **Lord, hear our prayer.**)

Leader: May the N......... family/household have a peace-filled and productive school year.

(The household named comes forward, adds their school symbol to the centerpiece *and places their piece of the group symbol.* Encourage families to word their petitions as prayers, e.g., "For our Aunt Lucy, we pray to the Lord"; not "I want to pray for . . .")

Leader: Lord, our God,

You are the source of all knowledge.

Keep us focused in our studies.

Help us to understand that all study is a prayer

And part of the way

We seek you.

We ask this in the name of Jesus.

All: Amen.

Closing

Leader: (Invite each family to come forward as their names are called and take back their school symbol *and their piece of the group symbol.*)

Leader: God, Source of all wisdom, bless the N...... family/household. Help them to study with diligence and work with patience during the upcoming school year.

Closing Song:

(Opening song or song appropriate to the lesson.)

Waiting
(Advent)

Preparation

There is no "at home" preparation for this ritual, but the leader can help the group prepare by asking them to quiet down and think about what it feels like to wait. Think of one word to describe that feeling. During the prayer, the leader is going to say "Waiting feels like . . ." and each person will be free to speak her word aloud. Parents could help little ones think of a word that describes the feeling of waiting.

Ritual

Opening Song:

Choose a gentle, Advent song, like "Patience, People," from the St. Louis Jesuits' *Calm Is the Night* album. Invite the group to listen to it.

Reader 1: "More than the watchman waits for the dawn, my soul waits for the Lord." Psalm 130:6

Reader 2: All of us wait.

Each day brings its own dose

Of waiting.

We wait

In dentists' offices,

At sports practices,

At school.

We wait for supper to be ready,

For the paper to be given back,

For the refund,

For the letter from a friend.

We wait

To be big enough to ride the roller coaster,

Old enough to stay up late,

Secure enough to be on our own.

Our waiting feels like. . . . (give people a chance to voice their feeling).

Advent calls us to celebrate waiting.

Each time we wait,

Help us to remember

How the world waited for a Savior.

Help us to remember

We are always waiting for Your return.

Help us to find and recognize You

In each other

As we wait.

We are an Advent people.

Family/Household:

Lord, the N....... family is waiting for you. (*As each family speaks this phrase, they come forward and place their piece of the symbol.*)

All: Come, Lord Jesus.

Song: "Come, Lord Jesus" by Carey Landry, or other gentle Advent song.

Possible Readings:

Habakkuk 2:2-3, Psalm 33:20-22, Psalm 130:5-6 Luke 2:26-38

Winter

Preparation

This is a ritual for places that experience snow in winter. Ask families to think about what snow means to them and to bring a symbol of winter to the meeting. They may want to bring paper snowflakes, shovels, mittens, hats, etc. If you have an old coat tree, it would make an excellent centerpiece for this prayer.

Ritual

Opening Song:

Any winter song.

Reader 1: "You are the maker of day and night,
You instituted light and sun,
You fixed the boundaries of the world,
You created summer and winter." Psalm 74:16-17

Reader 2: Winter,
The earth lies dormant,
The trees,
The seeds,
The animals,
Lie sleeping.
Long, dark nights,
Dwindling daylight
Turn our thoughts homeward,
To lighted windows
And blazing hearths.

Snow blankets the earth
Pretending
The world is pure -
And the children,
Those who *are* pure,
Slide on its surface
And delight in its newness.
Let the winter cold,
The treachery of ice,
The deceptiveness of snow
Remind us to look homeward.

Leader: God of winter and summer, help us to remember that life is cyclical. We need a dormant period to bring forth fruit. Teach us patience as we wait for spring. We ask this in the name of Jesus.

All: Amen

(The leader explains that the group will present the articles they have brought to the meeting and each will be described as a reason to praise God. For example, someone may present mittens and say, "For mittens, which protect our hands from the cold . . ." and the group will respond, "We praise you, Lord." Each of the articles will be added to the centerpiece.)

Leader: Let every season become a reminder to praise you, O Lord.

Song: Repeat Opening song

The Desert
(Lent)

Preparation

Ask each person to bring a rock to the meeting. If you are in an area that has no rocks, some sand. Ask each person to think of a fault they wish to give up for Lent. Some suggestions would be: busyness, not listening, impatience, anger, talking back, disrespect, unkindness, lying, etc. Prepare a centerpiece for prayer with a desert theme.

Ritual

Opening Song:

Any song with a Lenten, desert theme. "Come Back To Me" by Weston Priory, or something similar.

Reader 1: "The Spirit drove Jesus into the desert, and he remained there for forty days." Mark 1:12

Reader 2: Deserts

Are empty places,

Hot and dry in the glaring light of the sun,

Cold and desolate at night.

We are afraid of the desert.

We avoid the heat and the cold,

The loneliness,

But in the desert,

Stripped of the distractions,

The incidentals that crowd our days,

We are free

To discover ourselves

And meet our God.

Leader: Lord, our hearts grow cold as stone, dry as sand. Here in the desert, take away our stony hearts and give us hearts of flesh.

(Leader surrenders stone or sand to centerpiece and prays:)

Leader: Lord, this Lent, I surrender (give up) .... which makes my heart stony.

(Each of the people adds a stone or sand to the centerpiece and states the fault they wish to give up for Lent. *When everyone has surrendered a stone, one person from each household comes forward with their piece of the symbol and places it, saying: "Lord, help us to be present to you and to each other this Lent."*)

Leader: Loving God, forgive our faults. Take away our hearts of stone and give us new hearts. We ask this in the name of Jesus.

All: Amen.

Possible Readings:
Ezekiel 36:24-29, Luke 4:1-13

Desert

(alternative)

Preparation

This ritual can be extended into an entire lesson by giving the members of the group the opportunity to make sand paintings at the end of the prayer. Colored sand can usually be purchased at craft stores, and the paintings can be made in clear plastic glasses or baby food jars and sealed with melted wax.

Begin by asking the group to sit quietly and think about the images the word "desert" conveys.

Ritual

Opening Song:

Any song that reflects on the desert experience.

Reader 1: "I will turn the desert into pools of water and the dry land into flowing springs." Isaiah 41:18

Reader 2: The desert,

>> Empty,

>> Barren,

>> Lonely.

> What do you think of what you think of desert?

(Allow the members of the group to softly voice words that describe desert for them.)

> In times of plenty,

>> We forget about our need,

>> We forget about God.

We need the desert to remind us,

To strip us bare

Of all our distractions,

To focus us once again

On our purpose,

Our call,

Our God.

Leader: Jesus went to the desert to pray. It is important for each of us to create a quiet desert within, where we can be alone with God. It is the prayer of the desert that brings us back again to share with one another.

(*Members of the group come forward with their piece of the symbol, saying: "Help us to be present to God and to each other."*)

(If you are making sand paintings, begin playing quiet music, distribute materials and ask everyone to make a painting that reminds them of the prayerfulness of the desert.)

Closing

Leader: Often we are led

Into the desert,

But sometimes

We create our own desert

By forgetting

To nurture our dreams

And feed our aspirations,

By neglecting to drink deep

Of the waters of life.

(Families/households come forward to accept their symbol.)

Leader: N..., create a desert space within you and water *it with prayer.*

Family/Household:
> *We will*

Song: "Come to the Water" or a similar song about quenching thirst.

Possible Readings:
> Isaiah 41:17-18, Isaiah 44:3-4, Luke 4:1-13

New Life

(Easter/Spring)

Preparation

Ask families to take a walk and look for signs of new life in the world around them, bringing one sign to the meeting. The leader prepares a centerpiece with some signs of new life.

Ritual

Opening Song:

An Easter song.

Reader 1: "I am the resurrection and the life. All who believe in me, even if they die, will live forever." John 11:25

Reader 2: Winter has passed,
The earth struggles
To give birth.
Prepared by the barrenness,
Made fertile
By lying fallow,
The earth is ready.
We, too, have prepared
In silence,
In solitude,
In the Lenten desert.
May our preparation
Bring forth much fruit.

Leader: God of life, You promised us new life in and through Your Son. Open our hearts and alert our minds to the signs of that life.

(Leader calls forth one family/household/member at a time. All add their sign of new life to the centerpiece *and their pieces of the symbol to the group symbol,* while saying:)

Member: Open our eyes, Lord, to all the life You are calling forth in each of us.

All: Amen.

Leader: God of life, help us to celebrate this Easter season with joy, knowing that beyond every death there is new life.

All: Amen.

Song: Any Easter Song

Possible Readings:

Luke 24:13-35, John 21:1-23 or any of the Resurrection narratives.

Summer Vacation

Preparation

Ask each member to bring a symbol of vacation time. Family members may each want to bring an individual symbol. The leader should prepare a centerpiece with symbols of the school year.

Ritual

Opening Song:

A song that deals with new life or rest.

Reader 1: "Send forth your Spirit, Lord, and we shall be recreated."

Reader 2: Vacation,

Summer,

A time for recreation,

A time to be re-created.

A time to play.

A time to rest.

A time for empty space

In the crowded rush

Of our lives.

A time

For being renewed.

Leader: God who makes all things new, renew us through this vacation time. Rest our bodies and our spirits so that we may begin again, refreshed and renewed.

Many of us have worked hard in school, helping children in school, carpooling to sports, but our efforts are off-balance without time to be refreshed.

(Leader begins to change centerpiece by adding his symbol for vacation and saying:)

Leader: Thank you, God for ....

(Each of the members of the group do the same, adding symbols as they thank God for something specific about summer which the symbol represents. *If the group is assembling a symbol, this is done at the same time.*)

Leader: Let us pray for our special needs over the coming months.

(Spontaneous prayer of the faithful, to which the group responds, Lord, hear our prayer.)

Leader: Protect us, God of refreshment, throughout our vacation time, and let us never forget You. We ask this in the name of Jesus.

All: Amen.

Possible Reading:
Matthew 11:28-30

Rituals are Rooted in Symbols

The following rituals were designed specifically for use with the symbols given earlier in this book. The page where a specific symbol can be found is listed with each ritual. The rituals are not **limited** to this use only, however. Other groups of individuals, as well as intergenerational groups, will find the ritual adaptations simple and easy to follow. Groups using one symbol may choose a different ritual to awaken the community, stress a certain time of year or need in the group, or simply because they like a particular ritual.

Water

Preparation

This ritual was written to be used by those groups who use water as their symbol (see p. 55). It can be used by others simply by asking each household (or individual) to bring a small vial or bottle of water from their own home to the meeting. The leader prepares a centerpiece with a Bible, a candle, and a large clear container from which water can be easily poured.

Ritual

Opening Song:

Any song that deals with water, coming together, etc.

(Lower lights)

Reader 1: "In the beginning, God created the heavens and the earth. Now the earth was a formless void, there was darkness over the deep, and God's spirit hovered over the water." Genesis 1:1-2

Reader 2: Water,
Symbol of life.
We are born of water,
In birth and baptism,
We bless ourselves,
Bathe ourselves,
Refresh ourselves,
In water.
We stand awestruck before the ocean,

Powerless before the flood,

Breathless before the waterfall,

As water reminds us

Of the awesome presence of God.

(Leader invites members of each household to reverently hold up the water they have brought.)

Leader: Lord, you brought forth water from the rock,

You parted the sea

And calmed the storm.

Bless this water now,

Symbol of our very selves.

Let it mingle with the water of others

And bring forth new life.

(Each family/household/individual comes forward and pours water into the large container, saying the following prayer while pouring:)

Family: We, the N........, commit ourselves and our gifts to the life of the community. We pray especially today for . . . (any personal need may be mentioned).

All: Lord, hear our prayer.

Leader: Lord, make us one as the water in this vial has become one. Keep us attentive to You and to one another, and may this sharing bring forth new life.

All: Amen.

Closing

(The leader invites the group to reflect on the evening they have just shared, then calls each family forward, one by one, and refills their small vial while saying:)

Leader: N......, receive this water, symbol of your life in Christ, changed by the water with which it has mingled, by the community and the lives you have shared. Treasure the water as you treasure your community.

Family: Amen.

Closing Song:

Joyful, focus on water, baptism, community

Possible Readings:

Jeremiah 17:7-8, Isaiah 55:1-3, Isaiah 55:8-11, Isaiah 49:8-11, John 4:13-14, Isaiah 44:3-5

Wind

Preparation

This ritual was designed to be used by a group that has chosen to use the kite or wind chimes as its symbol. It can be used effectively in other groups by preparing people in advance. Each household (individual) makes a ribbon to be tied on the tail of the kite with their name and the gifts (done in pictures or words) which they feel they bring to the community. The leader needs to provide a kite, with a long tail for attaching the ribbon ties. Or the leader can provide a basic ring, and each household can be given a string of chimes, (see page 56), with a chime decorated for each person. (This prayer service can also provide an opening ritual for those who use a ship and sails for their symbol, p. 56.)

Ritual

Opening Song:

A song of the Spirit that speaks of the Spirit as wind or breath. "Wind Beneath My Wings" by Bette Midler is very appropriate, if you have access to it.

Reader 1: "Yahweh drove back the sea with a strong wind, and made the dry land appear." Exodus 14:22

Reader 2: Wind,

> Sometimes howling
>
> Across the earth,
>
> Shaking the very mountains
>
> With its power,
>
> Sometimes moving gently,
>
> Caressing the treetops,
>
> Ruffling the waters

90

As it whispers by.

We lift sails,

Erect windmills,

Hang wind chimes

In calculated attempts

To tap into

Its awesome power.

But we cannot harness the wind,

We cannot capture or contain it.

Like the Spirit,

It blows where it will.

(Invite each family to come forward to add their tie to the kite or their chimes to the wind chime ring.)

Family: Spirit-God, touch the N..... family and keep us attentive to Your touch and to one another. We pray especially for . . .

All: Hear us, O God.

Leader: Spirit-God, You blow where You will, giving power to our movement and music to our lives. Open us up to be always aware of Your presence and willing and able to respond. We ask this in the name of Jesus.

All: Amen.

Closing

(Leader calls each family or household forward, presenting them with their portion of the symbol.)

Leader: May the Spirit of God be present in the N.... family, as a powerful wind filling you with strength, a gentle breath, filling you with life.

All: Amen.

Possible Readings:

John 3:7-8, 1 Kings 18:45, Acts 2:1-4

Fire

Preparation

This ritual was prepared for those who use candles as symbols for their group (see p. 55). However, it can be used successfully with another group simply by inviting each household (or individual) to bring a candle to the group or by providing one. The leader prepares a centerpiece in which a candle figures prominently as the focus for the prayer, with a candle holder for each of the candles members will be bringing.

Ritual

Opening Song:

The opening song needs to focus on light. Anything from the camp song, "I've Got A Light," to something about Christ, the Light of the World, will work well. Lights are then extinguished. Reader 1 may read with a small flashlight.

Reader 1: "The people that walked in darkness

Have seen a great light.

On those who live in a land of deep shadow

A light has shown." Isaiah 9:1

(The leader lights the central candle.)

Reader 2: Fire,

Our physical assault

On the darkness.

No longer must we wait for the dawn,

For we are capable

Of bringing light

Into this darkness.
Fire,
Our commitment
To challenge the darkness
That threatens to envelop us,
For no amount of darkness
Can overcome
Our one, small flame.

(Leader calls each household/individual forward, one at a time, to light their candle and place it with the central candle. Each person/family recites while doing this:)

Family: Help us, Lord, to let your light shine within us and give light to others. Let your light shine especially on . . . (Household mentions any particular prayers).

All: God of Light, hear us.

Leader: Light a fire in our hearts, Lord, capable of consuming and transforming the earth. We ask this in the name of Jesus.

All: Amen.

Closing

(The leader calls each of the families forward, one at a time, and hands each a lighted candle.)

Leader: N....., the light is within you.

(Family blows out the candle.)

Possible Readings:
John 1:1-5, Isaiah 9:1-4

Rainbows

Preparation

This ritual is most effectively celebrated outside, in daylight. When this is the case, have every household/individual bring "bubble stuff" and a wand. It can be done effectively inside by creating an arc of the rainbow for each household (see p. 53).

Ritual

Opening Song:

Any rainbow song.

Reader 1: "God said, 'Here is the sign of the Covenant I make between Myself and you and every living creature with you for all generations: I set my bow in the clouds and it shall be a sign of the Covenant between Me and the earth.'" Genesis 9: 12-13

Reader 2: Rainbows,

God's promise to the earth.

God, Who is light,

Has passed through our existence,

Bending to us

To reveal the colors,

The beauty

Of divine love.

We, too, are called

To be rainbows for others,

Refracting the divine,

Revealing the colors of God's love,
As the light passes through us.

*****

(If the ritual takes place outside, the leader makes a bubble with the wand and says softly as it rises:)

Leader: Help me to be a rainbow for others.

(Leader invites group members to do the same.)

*   *   *

(If the ritual takes place inside, each family/household comes forward, placing their arc in the rainbow and saying:)

Family: God, help us to be present to each other this evening, so that together we may fully reflect the beauty of your love.

All: Amen.

*   *   *

Leader: You have called us Lord, to be a rainbow people, filled with light, reflecting Your love. May our time together create rainbows in each of our hearts. We ask this in the name of Jesus.

All: Amen.

Closing

Leader: N......., be true to the color God calls you to be and carry the rainbow of God's promise in your heart.

(While saying these words, the leader hands each household/family/individual their arc.)

Possible Readings:
Genesis 9:12-16, Revelations 4:1-3

Time

Preparation

 This prayer service can be used with the sundial symbol or a leader can have each household/individual bring a small amount of sand in a little glass jar. (Baby food jars work well.) The leader supplies a fairly large vase with a small opening and a funnel, clear if possible. (This will make a makeshift hourglass. The opening in the funnel can be made smaller by putting tape around the inside. Make sure there is no stickiness on the outside of the tape, since this could cause the funnel to clog.) The leader makes a centerpiece around the makeshift hourglass or the central piece of the sundial. (Also, see p. 57.)

Ritual

Opening Song:

Any song that focuses on "time": "A Time Will Come For Singing," from the St. Louis Jesuits, "For Everything A Season," or any time song.

Reader 1: "There is a season for everything, a time for every occupation under heaven." Ecc 3:1

Reader 2: Time,

> It marks its quiet passage
> Through our days and nights.
> We speak of "having" it,
> "Saving" it, "spending" it,
> "Using" it or "wasting" it,
> Perhaps, even "giving" it.
> But it is all illusion;

It was never ours.
It slips through our lives
As sand through the hourglass,
As sun across the sky.
We have only the moment,
The Now,
The time in which to build
The timeless eternal.

Leader: Eternal God, we place the time, our past and our future, in Your hands. Help us to be present in the Now, to fill each moment with Your love, one moment at a time.

(Leader pours sand into makeshift hourglass or adds piece to the sundial.)

Leader: I relinquish my attempt to control time and ask You, God, to help me to be truly present to You, to others, and especially to . . . (mentions any special need).

All: Listen to our prayer.

(Each family/household repeats the action. If you have very young children in the group, change the word "relinquish" to "let go of." Children do not attempt to control time anyway, but that is a very big word for them.)

Closing

The leader gives each family/individual their piece of the sundial or pours sand back into their jar, saying:

Leader: N......, receive this time as a gift. Give yourselves fully to each moment and to everything that touches your lives.

All: Amen.

Possible Readings:
Ecclesiastes 3:1-8, Mark 1:14-15, Matthew 6:25-34, John 9:4-5

The Cross

Preparation

This ritual can be used with any of the symbols based on the cross (see p. 54), or without any group symbol. It can be very unifying for a group to present all of the members with small wooden crosses to be worn as a symbol of their Christian faith and their commitment to the community. A ritual for presenting crosses is given as the closing of this particular prayer.

Ritual

Opening Song:

Although the symbol of this ritual is the cross, the theme is really following Jesus. "I Have Decided to Follow Jesus" or any song that emphasizes following Jesus will work well.

Reader 1: "If any of you want to be a follower of mine, you must renounce yourself and take up your cross and follow me." Mark 8:34

Reader 2: Three crosses
> Standing empty on a hill,
> Not just a sign
> Of suffering and death,
> But of new life.
> Their beams stretch upward
> Toward heaven,
> Outward
> Toward earth,
> A stark reminder

That suffering calls us

To reach upward

(Or downward)

Toward God,

And outward

Toward each other,

That our pain

Might also lead

To new life.

Leader: God of goodness, we are bound together in our weakness, bonded by our pain. Help us always to reach out to one another. (Adding his piece of the cross symbol, the leader says:)

Help me to be aware of the needs of my community and my world, particularly the needs of . . . (leader prays for personal intentions; group responds: **"Hear us, O God**.)

(Each household/individual adds piece to the symbol. If the group is not using a symbol, a simple prayer of the faithful can be added here, with particular attention to those who are suffering.)

Leader: Help us, O God of the weak, as we take up our cross to follow You.

All: Amen.

Closing

Leader: N...., receive this cross *(piece of the cross, candle from the cross)* as a sign of your commitment to Christ, your community and the world.

All: Amen.

Possible Readings:

Mark 8:34-36, Luke 9:23-26, Isaiah 43:1-3

Circles

Preparation

This ritual was designed to be used with groups using concentric circles as a symbol (see p. 53). This symbol can be created for the meeting by making the circles in advance out of cardboard, giving each member (family) a circle, and asking them to prepare by decorating it for the next meeting. The ritual can also be done without the symbol.

You may want to begin by asking a child to demonstrate the motion of the earth. Once he is standing and spinning, ask another child to be the sun. Direct your spinning earth to travel around the sun. Ask the sun to begin to travel around the room with the earth still spinning circles around it. The group can then imagine the room spinning on its own orbit. This gives a graphic picture of the circles of our universe.

Ritual

Opening Song:

The theme of this prayer is both unity and eternity. Any song that focuses on one of these themes will work. Have everyone join hands in a circle for the song. (Keep the song simple so that members don't need to be holding words.)

Reader 1: "God, who lives above the circle that is the earth . . . has stretched out the heavens like a cloth, spread them like a tent for humanity to live in." Isaiah 40:22

Reader 2: We live on a spinning circle,

Travelling in circles around the sun,

In a solar system that circles within a galaxy,

In a galaxy that circles in a universe.

The circle,

No beginning,

No end,

A constant reminder

Of the eternity of God.

Circular motion,

Finding the source of its energy

In the center,

A constant reminder

Of our own needs.

We are connected within that circle,

Dependent on one another

To be complete,

To present the true image of God.

Leader: God of no beginning and end, source of our strength and our motion, help us to be connected to You and to one another. We ask this in the name of Jesus.

All: Amen.

(If the group is assembling a symbol, each family/household would come forward, one at a time, add their piece to the symbol and say:)

Member: We, the N........ family, are a circle within circles, dependent on God and on one another for our strength. Tonight, Lord, we especially pray . . . (mentions any special need).

All: Lord, hear our prayer.

Leader: God of no beginning and end, hear and answer the prayers of those united in the circle of Your love.

Closing

Leader presents each household with a piece of the circle, saying:

Leader: N.......family, let this circle remind you of your Center and your community.

All: Amen.

Possible Readings:
John 14:1-4, 1 John 1-4

Stars

Preparation

There is no preparation to be done at home for this lesson. If you are assembling a star, members need to bring their pieces (see p. 54). Whether or not you are using a symbol, you may want to begin by asking the group what they think of when they think of a star. If this ritual will be repeated each time the group meets, ask them to come back each time with a different idea of "star."

Ritual

Opening Song:

Any song that deals with stars, any kind, or a song about light.

Reader 1: "We have seen His star in the East and have come to adore the Lord." Matt 2:2

Reader 2: It was a sign,
And only the wise ones
Recognized it.
Have we seen His star?
Are we willing to set aside
Our lives,
Our wealth,
Our own "stardom"
To follow His star?
Have we seen it in the East?

Leader: God, Who placed the stars in the heavens and chose one to alert us to the birth of Your Son, grant us the wisdom always to watch for Your signs. Help us to respond with our gifts. We ask this in the name of Jesus.

All: Amen.

(Each of the members or households comes forward one at a time and assembles the star, saying:)

Member: We, the N......family, will always try to follow Your star.

Closing

Leader calls each family forward, presents them with their piece of the symbol and says:

Leader: N...., carry the light of Christ in your hearts.

Song: (Any light song)

Bibliography

Bell, Catherine. *Ritual Theory, Ritual Practice.* New York: Oxford University Press, 1992.

Benson, Jeanette and Hilyard, Jack L. *Becoming Family.* Winona, MN: St. Mary's College Press, 1978.

Covert, Anita and Thomas, Gordon L. *Communication, Games and Simulations.* Salem, OR: Eric Clearinghouse, 1978.

DeGidio, Sandra. *Enriching Faith through Family Celebrations.* Mystic, CT: Twenty-Third Publications, 1989.

Dillistone, F.W. *The Power of Symbol in Religion and Culture.* New York: Crossroad, 1986.

Forbess-Greene, Sue. *The Encyclopedia of Icebreakers.* Applied Skills Press, 1983.

Foster, Elizabeth Sabrinsky. *Energizers and Icebreakers: For All Ages and Stages.* Minneapolis: Educational Media Corp., 1989.

Kraus, Richard G. *The Family Book of Games.* Hightstown: McGraw-Hill, 1960.

Krueger, Caryl Waller. *1001 Things to Do with your Kids.* Nashville: Abingdon Press, 1988.

Martos, Joseph. *Doors to the Sacred.* Garden City: Doubleday, 1982.

Meyer, Jerome Sydney. *The Big Book of Family Games: The Most Complete Treasury of Fun-Filled Games and Activities for Family and Friends.* Los Angeles: Galahad Books, 1974.

Peck, M. Scott. *The Different Drum.* New York: Simon and Schuster, 1987.

Ripley, Sherman. *Book of Games.* Chicago: Association Press, 1952.

Stein, Lincoln David. *Family Games.* New York: Macmillan, 1979.

Stuart, Sally E. *100 Plus Party Games: Fun and Easy Ideas for Parties & Holidays.* Santa Fe, Bear & Co., 1988.

Winter, Miriam Therese. *God With Us: Resources for Prayer and Praise.* Nashville: Abingdon, 1979.

Wiswell, Phil. *I Hate Charades and 49 Other New Games.* New York: Sterling Publishers, 1981.

Other books by Kathy Chesto:

- *Why Are The Dandelions Weeds? Stories for Growing Faith*
- *Risking Hope: Fragile Hope in the Healing Process*
- *Family-Centered Intergenerational Religious Education* (4-year program for in-home religious education)
- *Children's Scripture Puzzles* (weekly, scripture-related puzzles for Cycles A, B, and C; in 3 volumes)